Green Fingers

& GREEN SCREEN

SANDRA WOODCOCK • IRIS HOWDEN

Published in association with The Basic Skills Agency

Hodder & Stoughton

A MEMBE   ROUP

Order queries: Please contact Bookpoint Ltd, 39 Milton Park, Abingdon, Oxon OX14 4TD. Telephone: (44) 01235 400414. Fax: (44) 01235 400454. Lines are open from 9 am - 6 pm Monday to Saturday, with a 24-hour message answering service. Email address: orders@bookpoint.co.uk

The publishers and The Basic Skills Agency wish to acknowledge the contribution of the NEWNAT Project, Nottinghamshire LEA, and of the Project Leader, Peter Beynon, in the conception, writing and publication of the series.

A CIP record is available from the British Library

ISBN 0 340 52102 3

First published 1989
New edition 1996
Impression number   17 16 15 14 13 12 11 10 9 8
Year   2004 2003 2002 2001 2000 1999 1998

Copyright © 1989, 1996 The Basic Skills Agency

Typeset by Gecko Limited, Bicester, Oxon.
Printed in Great Britain for Hodder & Stoughton Educational, a division of Hodder Headline Plc, 338, Euston Road, London NW1 3BH by Redwood Books, Trowbridge, Wiltshire BA14 8RN.

Green Fingers

When Bill retired everyone told him to keep busy.
'You'll need a hobby,' they said.
'Time hangs heavy when you're at home.'
'Days seem to get longer as you get older,'
said his retired friends.
But Bill knew all this.
He had a hobby.
It was something he'd been doing for years.
Now with all this time to himself
he could really get on with it.

Bill had always loved growing things.
He'd never had a garden, only a backyard.
But he had a small greenhouse there.
When he had worked at the factory
he'd not had much time for his plants.
So his hobby hadn't been a problem
for his wife, Winnie.
But now she was really fed up.

1

All spring and summer
Bill had been busy with his plants.
The greenhouse was full.
Great big flowerpots lined up
against the wall of the yard.
Long, lanky plants looked down on her
when she put out her washing.
From hanging baskets
other plants put out long arms.
Leaves dangled over the door,
swinging in the wind.
Around the kitchen window
something was creeping up a trellis.

But Winnie didn't share
Bill's love for plants.
'They're all right in their place,'
she grumbled to her sister.
'I've never minded a nice plant
on the window sill.
But Bill! Now he's gone too far.
It's not just the plants.
It's everything!
I thought when Bill retired
we could enjoy life a bit.
I thought we would go out more ... trips to the
sea-side ... you know.
But really he's not much fun at all.

2

She grumbled to Bill as well –
loud and long.
She nagged him. She mocked him.
'Why don't you grow something useful
if we must have these pots around?
What about tomatoes?
Jack Fisher – now he grows lovely tomatoes.
His wife tells me she never buys salad in the shops.
Lovely lettuces in growbags he's got.
You think more about these plants than me.
Why don't you spend a bit of money on *me*
for a change?'

Bill said nothing.
He went on sorting out his new compost,
extra pots and packets of seeds.
The yard was now a mass of green leaves,
twisting stems and bright flowers.

'You should be pleased,' said Bill.
'Plenty of women would love a garden like this.'
'Looks like a jungle!' said Winnie.
'It only wants a few parrots
and it would be just like a jungle!'

And so they went on.
Winnie couldn't say a good word about his hobby.
Bill was so stubborn about it.
He was going to carry on
whether she liked it or not.

At last there was no more room in the yard.
Not even Bill could find a space
to put the smallest pot or hanging basket.
'Good,' said Winnie to herself.
'He'll have to stop now.'
But to her dismay Bill took his hobby indoors –
indoor plants! This was even worse!
Winnie felt as if she was being pushed
into a smaller and smaller corner of her home.

Bill fussed over the plants.
He looked on them as dear friends.
He talked to them of course.
All the best gardeners do.
He had less and less time for Winnie.
She wished he was back at work again.

One day when he was out,
Winnie felt something snap inside her.
A fit of rage gripped her.
She swept her arm along the window sill
and knocked six plants on to the carpet.
Then she swung round.
She tipped over the coffee table with
three more plants on it.
She pulled a trailing plant
from a bracket on the wall.
She snapped three leaves off a big
Swiss Cheese plant in the corner.
Then she stopped.

The room was very still and quiet.

But there seemed to be another anger there now
as well as her own.
The plants lay on the floor.
Their white roots were exposed.
They looked like the sad victims of a crime.
Other plants, ones she hadn't touched,
seemed to stare at her.
Winnie's legs felt weak.
She sat down.
A long stem of a hanging plant touched her face.
She brushed it away with her hand.
It dangled on the back of her neck.

***

9

When Jean came to see her sister
she found Winnie on the floor.
She knew at once that she was dead.

The policeman said Winnie had been strangled.
He thought some kind of string had been used.
But he could not find any.
She must have put up a struggle.
The broken plant pots and coffee table showed that
But there was no sign of a break-in.
Nothing was stolen.
It was a real mystery.
Bill had a good alibi.
He'd been helping the two gardeners
in the local park all day.

Winnie's death made the headlines in the paper.
Everyone felt sorry for Bill.
But he soon settled down to life on his own.
He had his plants to fuss over.
Now, more than ever, they seemed like friends –
especially the one on top of the bookcase
with its long dangling stems,
reaching into the room like fingers . . .

11

Green Screen

Sue was fed up.
She spent every night on her own watching T.V.
There was nothing good on tonight.
She might as well have an early night.
On her way to bed
she looked in at the study.
She put her head round the door.
'I'm off to bed,' she said.
'Right, Sue. See you later.' Tony didn't look up.
His eyes were fixed
on the green screen in front of him.
His fingers moved quickly over the keyboard.
Rows of figures appeared in lines across the screen.
Sue shut the door
and went away without saying another word.
There was no use talking to him.
He lived in a world of his own.

Things came to a head a few weeks later.
Tony had taken to working on his computer
right into the night.
Sue would often wake in the early hours
to find him gone.

He was going back to the study
to carry on with his work.
'What are you doing that's so important?'
she asked.
'Can't you do it at work?'
Tony looked at her in a funny way.
'What do you mean, work?' he said.
'Who told you it was for the firm?
It's much more important than that.'
Sue was worried.
'That computer's taking him over,' she thought.

Then Sue had an idea.
She asked Bob and Angie round to dinner.
She took a lot of trouble cooking the meal.
The table was set out
with the best china, flowers and candles.
Things were going well
when Tony suddenly left the room.
Twenty minutes later he still hadn't come back.
'Should I go and look for him?' Bob asked.
'Maybe he's feeling ill.'
Bob went upstairs.
He came back ten minutes later.
'Tony's got some work to finish
on the computer,' he said.
'Are you sure he's not overdoing it, Sue?
Maybe you should get him to see a doctor.'

Bob and Angie left early.

As soon as they had gone, Sue ran upstairs.

'How could you do this to me?' she shouted.

Tony didn't hear her.

His eyes were fixed on the screen.

It was glowing with a bright green light.

Words flashed on and off.

'MORE INFORMATION' it said

on the green screen.

'MORE INFORMATION'.

Tony's fingers moved quickly over the keys.

Lines of figures sped across the screen.

'Can't you hear me?' she yelled.

'Stop it! I'm talking to you!'

Tony didn't answer.

He went on typing faster and faster.

Sue lost her temper.

'Stop!' she shouted. 'Listen. I've had enough.'

She reached over for the 'OFF' switch.

Tony turned round.

His face was white with rage.

'You stupid bitch!

Don't you dare touch that switch.'

He got up and pushed her through the door.

'Get out and stay out!' he shouted.

Sue made up her mind to leave him.
She'd go to her mother's for a few days –
give him time to think things over.
She was sure that he'd miss her
and ask her back.
But he didn't.

After a few weeks
Sue knew that he wasn't going to phone.
Whatever he was doing
was more important to him than his wife.
She wondered what it could be.
What was he typing night after night?
Had he become a spy?
Was he selling information to another firm?
'No, that's daft,' she thought.

Then she had a call from Mrs Hill,
their next door neighbour.
Mrs Hill was worried about Tony.
She hadn't seen him for days.

'I know he's in the house,' Mrs Hill said.
'The light's on all night.
But we haven't seen Tony.
His car's in the garage,
and I'm sure he's not going to work.
I thought you should know.'
Sue went straight round to the house.
Everything was in darkness – apart from one light,
the light in Tony's study.

She felt afraid. What was wrong?
Had Tony been taken ill?
He might have had a heart attack.
She shouldn't have left him.
She took out her key and let herself in.
The house was in a terrible state.
There were books and papers everywhere.
She ran upstairs to the study.
What would she find?

As she reached the door
she heard the tap, tap, tap of the plastic keys.
Nothing had changed.
Tony was still working on that bloody computer.

Then she saw Tony. What a shock!
He was so thin and pale.
He looked as if he hadn't eaten for weeks.
His clothes were filthy and he needed a shave.
His blood-shot eyes stared out at the screen.
All the time
his fingers moved to and fro over the keys,
never stopping.
And all the time,
the same words flashed across the screen –
'MORE INFORMATION' . . .
'MORE INFORMATION'.

'Tony, stop!' she begged.
'You're killing yourself.'
But Tony sat like someone in a dream –
typing, typing, typing . . .

Sue ran to the phone.
Ten minutes later the ambulance came.
The ambulance men tried
to get Tony away from the computer.
He fought like a mad-man.
In the end they had to give him an injection
to calm him down.
Tony lay on the floor,
his eyes fixed on the green screen.
His hands reached up as if to go on typing.
When they put him into the ambulance
he began to cry like a baby.

Sue went back to get Tony's things.
He would need pyjamas, slippers and so on.
She went towards the bathroom
to fetch his shaving gear.
As she passed the study she heard a buzzing sound.
Of course – the computer.
Well, she'd got Tony away from it at last.

She would enjoy switching it off.
Tony would soon get better.
All he needed was rest.
She went into the room.
The screen was brighter then ever.
The same words flashed across:
'MORE INFORMATION'.
They seemed to hold her eyes.
She couldn't look away.
She felt herself being pulled towards the computer.

Her hands reached out.
They no longer belonged to her.
Her fingers moved onto the keyboard.
She sat down like someone in a dream.
Then she began to type . . .